Parenting Plan

Preparation is Key

Michele Sfakianos, RN, BSN

Open Pages Publishing, LLC
P.O. Box 61048
Fort Myers, FL 33906
http://www.my411books.com
(239) 454-7700

Parenting Plan

ISBN 9780996068758

This book is dedicated to all parents who wish to raise strong, confident, and well-prepared young adults.

Acknowledgments

Thank you to everyone who continues to support my writing. I am fortunate to live my passion to help others.

Thank you to my family and friends for encouraging me to share this information with you.

Introduction

Good parenting helps foster empathy, honesty, self-reliance, self-control, kindness, cooperation, and cheerfulness. It also promotes intellectual curiosity, motivation, and desire to achieve. It helps protect children from developing anxiety, depression, eating disorders, anti-social behavior, and alcohol and drug abuse.

Parenting is one the most researched areas in the entire field of social science. A parent's relationship with his or her child will be reflected in the child's actions – including behavior problems. If you don't have a good relationship with your child, they're not going to listen to you. Think how you relate to other adults. If you have a good relationship with them, you tend to trust them more, listen to their opinions, and agree with them. If it's someone we just don't like, we will ignore their opinion.

For positive child-rearing outcomes, the following skill areas are utilized:

1.   Love and affection: You support and accept the child, are physically affectionate and spend one-on-one time together. What you do matters!

2.   Stress management: You take steps to reduce stress for yourself and your child, practice relaxation techniques and promote positive interpretations of events.

3.   Relationship skills: You maintain a healthy relationship with your spouse, significant other, or co-parent and model effective relationship skills of events.

4.   Autonomy and independence: You treat your child with respect and encourage him or her to become self-sufficient and self-reliant. Keep pace with your child's development. Your child is growing up. Consider how age is affecting the child's behavior.

5.   Education and learning: You promote and model learning and provide educational opportunities for your child.

6.   Life skills: You manage your money responsibly, have a steady income, provide all household necessities for your child consistently and plan for the future. You teach your children responsible life skills starting at an early age.

7.   Behavior management: You make extensive use of positive reinforcement and punish only when other methods of managing behavior have failed. Be consistent. When parents aren't consistent, children get confused.

8.   Health: You model a healthy lifestyle and good habits, such as regular exercise and proper nutrition. Remember – you don't send the kids out to play, you go outside and play with them.

9.   Religion: You support spiritual or religious development and participate in spiritual or religious activities.

10. Safety: You take precautions to protect your child and maintain awareness of your child's activities and friends. Be involved in your child's life. Being an involved parent takes time and is hard work, and often means rethinking and rearranging your priorities.

There are so many things that we need to teach our children before they leave home and its best if we can start early. What life offers can change daily. There's a lot for them to keep up with today like technology, school, work, etc. Why not make the road ahead an easier one? The more they know about life skills the less they will have to learn the hard way.

The good news is, all of the parenting skills can be learned and improved upon through a variety of mediums, including: books, videos, parenting classes, coaching and/or counselors. The first step is yours to take and you are well on your way with this information!

Table of Contents

Chapter 1 – What's Your Parenting Style?

"It's no use saying, "We are doing our best." You have got to succeed in doing what is necessary."
Winston Churchill

What a difficult life a child leads today. Are our children forced to live on the edge at a superficial level with no acceptance and minimal positive affirmation from parents? Is the peer pressure too much? Are they learning to live from the Internet and television with no emphasis on moral values or excellence? Are you comfortable with your parenting style? Or, do you need to tweak some things? Only you can answer these questions.

Raising children in today's world is a tough challenge. After all, kids don't come with an instruction manual. New parent's often feel helpless and you must take comfort in knowing that this is a natural, very normal, response.

Parenting Styles

A parenting style involves a child rearing behavior (of parents, guardians, or other primary caregivers) that involves the amount of control over a child's activities and behavior and the degree of nurturance of the child. Parents can create their own styles from a combination of factors, and these can change over time as the children develop their own personalities and move through life's stages. Is there one style that works best for all children? No. Parenting styles are affected by both the parents' and child's temperaments and is largely based on the influence of one's own parents and culture. Most people learn parenting practices from their own parents. These parents can decide to accept or discard those practices.

Types of parenting styles, a sample of the top five:

1. Authoritative: These parents demand and respond, as character-ized by a child-centered approach, and hold high expectations of maturity for the child. Typical traits of authoritative parents:

- Warm and responsive and strive toward meeting their chil-dren's physical and emotional needs.
- Provide rules and guidance without being overbearing.
- Offer relative freedom of choice by encouraging independ-ent thinking and give-and-take discussions.
- Will forgive and teach, instead of punishing the child if he or she falls short.
- Were raised in a spirit of disciplined conformity, general obedience, and adherence to rules. Basically, the children do what they are told to do.
- Produce children who are more independent and self-reliant.

2. Indulgent or Permissive Parenting: These parents respond but do not demand. Also called lenient and are characterized as having few behavioral expectations for the child. Typical traits of indulgent parents:

- Meet the child's needs and are warm, responsive, and caring.
- Do not require children to regulate themselves.
- Use a nonrestrictive child-discipline strategy.
- Tend to evade conflicts, embrace harmony, and encourage give-and-take discussions.
- Encourage independent thinking.

3. Christian Parenting: These parents use the application of Biblical principles on parenting. Some Christian parents follow a strict and more authoritarian interpretation of the Bible, and others are "grace-based" and share other methods. Typical traits of Christian parents:

- Teach their children about formalized religion and religious practices.
- Teach children to memorize and meditate on scripture.
- Nourish their children with wholesome discipline and encourage them to build a personal relationship with God and to live a Christian life.
- Teach their children about forgiveness.
- Adhere to a clean life free of drugs, smoking, and other outside temptations.
- Encourage honesty and truthfulness.

4. Attachment Parenting or Natural Parenting: These parents seek to create a strong emotional bond and avoid physical punishment. Typical traits of attachment or natural parents:

- Seek to create a special bond.
- Respond with sensitivity.
- Practice positive discipline. Parents are encouraged to work out a solution together with a child, rather than spanking or simply imposing their will on the child.
- Strive for balance in personal and family life. Parents are encouraged to create a support network, live a healthy lifestyle, and prevent parenting burnout.

5. Helicopter Parenting: Helicopter parents keep their children at close range; always "hovering" above them, trying to make sure no harm will come to them. Typical traits of helicopter parents:

- Helicopter parents don't believe their children can take care of themselves, and they fear that if they don't keep tight control over everything, harm will come to their children.
- Often over-program their children and fail to allow them free time to play and explore on their own.
- Well known in the school system.
- Will complete basic tasks for their children, such as: homework, job applications, and college applications.
- Will try to solve all of their problems and sweep all obstacles out of the way.

Other parenting styles:

- Authoritarian: Parents that demand but do not respond (Strict Parenting), characterized by high expectations on conformity and compliance to parental rules and directions, while allowing little open dialogue between parent and child.
- Positive Parenting: Positive parenting works to empower children.
- Conscious Parenting or Unconditional Parenting: These parents show unconditional love rather than conditionally. They are against positive reinforcement parenting, meaning if the child behaves, the parent will show him love, and if he doesn't, the parent will not show him love.
- Slow Parenting: This style encourages parents to plan and organize less for their children, instead allowing them to enjoy their childhood and explore the world at their own pace.

- Negligent or Uninvolved Parenting: Neglectful parenting neither demands nor responds, also called hands-off parenting. The parents are low in responsiveness and do not set limits.
- Nurturant Parenting: A family model where children are expected to explore their surroundings with the protection of their parents.
- Narcissistic Parenting: These parents thirst for external recognition and acceptance and unconsciously use their children as a means to live out dreams and fantasies they never got to realize.
- Toxic Parenting: These parents range from children's needs to direct physical, emotional, and sometimes even sexual abuse.
- Shared Parenting: This style results when married parents equally share the responsibility of parenting and the responsibility of earning money.
- Punishment-based Parenting: These parents use pain, punishment, intimidation, yelling, degradation, humiliation, shame, guilt, or other things to hurt a child's self-esteem, or they hurt them physically. Punishment-based parenting also damages the relationship between the parent and child. It puts unnecessary pressure on the child, and the child is less apt to perform due to pressure.

No one parenting style is right or wrong. Parenting is a lifelong job of trials and errors, and hindsight is always 20/20. All parents must decide for themselves how to raise their children. There are no fixed rules, no written instructions, and no child manual. There are situations in all of our lives that influence the way we do things, both consciously and subconsciously. The way we were raised, and the time and place we were raised in, are all factors that play an important role in how we raise our children. Parents should keep an open mind to the choices other parents make, learning about the parenting styles of other cultures, and consider if there are things we should all do differently. No two kids are alike. What works for one child may not work for another. Find what works for your child.

Self-Discovery Challenge:

Of the parenting styles listed, which do you feel you utilize? Why?

Are there other parenting styles you weren't aware of until now? Will you try them?

How does your parenting style differ from how you were treated as a child?

Chapter 2 – Positive Parenting Behaviors

"There should never be any yelling in the home unless there is a fire."
David O. McKay

Most parents first experience their child's attempts at autonomy at about age two. It's the power struggle. They feel challenged and often a battle of wills begins that lasts throughout childhood and the teen years. Parents can turn these trying times into a rewarding growth period for them and their children by shifting their perspective concerning the child's behavior and by becoming clever and creative in responding to the child's perceived "headstrong, rebellious, stubborn, frustrating, negative" behavior.

Positive parenting, sometimes called positive discipline, gentle guidance, or loving guidance, is simply guidance that keeps our kids on the right path, offered in a positive way that resists any temptation to be punitive. Studies show that's what helps kids learn consideration and responsibility, and makes for happier kids and parents.

As parents, guardians, or caregivers, we should all be taking the following actions:

- Be yourself.
- Love and respect yourself and others.
- Listen respectfully to one another.
- Build the lines of communication. Always communicate in a positive manner. Never give them an "I told you so" response. Let them know they can talk to you about anything.

- Keep an open and nonjudgmental atmosphere.
- Address conflict in a positive manner.
- Do things and go places together.
- Show affection to one another comfortably.
- Have respect for everyone's personal space.
- Be flexible.
- Shed anger and bitterness.
- Be honest.
- Be patient.
- Keep your sense of humor.
- Compromise.
- Be understanding.
- Show unconditional love.
- Remember to enjoy your kids.
- Assist your children with their homework, but don't DO the homework.
- Keep the spark in your marriage. Spend time together away from the children.
- Encourage a relationship between the children and their biological parent, not living with them, if in a "step" relationship.
- Include the children in the moving details, decorating and home needs.
- Explain to the children (if of age to understand), the financial situation of the family.
- Establish core family values and live by them. Establish rules, set limits, and ensure conformity to those rules and limits.
- Make new memories in different ways.
- Be their parent, their moral compass, their guide, not their friend. Children emulate those they know best.
- Encourage your child to be an individual, not a follower, and encourage independence.

- Take responsibility for what you expose your small children and teens to daily. (TV, movies, video games)
- Monitor television, computers, cell phones, and other communication devices. Set and reinforce limits on your child's media use. Watch TV and movies together to better connect and discuss the messages sent about body image and other expectations.
- Provide a healthy and complete meal and sit down together as a family to enjoy it. Use mealtime to talk about things going on in each other's lives.
- Respect his or her opinion and take into account his or her thoughts and feelings. It's important your child knows you are listening.
- Engage in active listening. Active listening is a communication technique that requires the listener to understand, interpret, and evaluate what is heard. Once you hear your child's concerns, you will be able to feel what he or she feels. Active listening gives the child the opportunity to correct you. In other words: they talk, you listen, and you paraphrase what they said to you, and they tell you if you are correct. Doing so helps to fix any misunderstandings.
- Be honest and direct when talking about sensitive subjects such as sex, drugs, drinking, and smoking.
- Children want the chance to be trusted. Give them a chance.
- Be willing to admit you don't know everything and that you're not always right.
- Provide a supportive and encouraging environment. Focus on the positive, instead of criticizing, praise their special talents, and nurture their interests. Children want their parents to be proud of them.
- Children need their home to be a refuge, a safe haven.

- Model and teach positive stress management and coping skills. Children need help managing the stresses and pressure in their lives.
- Know your kid's friends.
- Never shame them when you find out something you don't approve of. Even "good" kids act out once in a while.
- Help your small children and teens build their self-esteem by teaching them techniques of goal achievement. Have them break down their big goals into small, achievable goals in order to alleviate some of the stress in their lives.
- Look out for signs of stress, anxiety, lack of concentration, poor food and drink intake, personal hygiene changes, sleep disturbances, lack of interest in social activities, and then address them immediately.
- Keep the medicine cabinet locked. Unlocked medicine cabinets are an open invitation for kids and their friends to abuse prescription drugs.
- Know that addiction runs in families and be proactive to prevent it.
- Know that addiction is a health problem and can be treated.
- Understand alcohol, tobacco, and substance abuse is preventable.
- Understand there's no shame in accepting professional help.

Positive Parenting is the approach to parenting that we believe best supports all aspects of healthy child development. It is based on decades of research into the links between parenting and how young children respond to life's challenges.

The best way to improve behavior is to give children a lot of attention when they are doing something you like and remove your attention when they are doing something you do not like. It's hard to get into the practice of doing this at first, but with time it gets easier.

Self-Discovery Challenge:

How do you feel about giving positive praise? How often do you give positive praise?

Of the positive praise items listed, are there others you could incorporate to your everyday interaction with your child?

How often do you engage in active listening? Will you use this technique more?

Chapter 3 – Negative Parenting Behaviors

"Those who look for the bad in people will surely find it."
Abraham Lincoln

We all intuitively know the way a child is parented has a deep and indelible impact on that child's life. But now, thanks to ever-more-detailed brain scans and scientific research, we're learning just how important parenting actually is. What happens during a child's formative years directly impacts the brain's growth and development…and not always for the better.

When a parent's behavior does not create a loving, supportive environment, a child's brain develops in altered form. Dysfunctional, irrational, and destructive behavior patterns are literally programmed into the child's brain, setting the stage for recurring issues throughout that child's life.

We've discussed the things you should be doing. Below are the things you should NOT do:

- Argue with a child.
- Be intrusive (unless you think there is a problem which could escalate into a horrific event.)
- Judge.
- Criticize.
- React out of emotion.
- Force the new relationship, if in a "step" child situation.

- Choose sides.
- Be quick to jump to conclusions.
- Try to reason with an angry child.
- Give consequences or punishment in the heat of the moment.
- Make threats in the heat of the moment.
- Lose sight of your family goals and values.
- Miss out on important milestones in your child's life. (Recital, sporting game, awards presentation, etc.)
- Let the ex-partner be dependent on you.
- Keep the children from their biological parent (unless it is a court-order or in the best interest of the child.)
- Keep the children from their grandparents (both maternal and paternal).
- Fight with your partner, your ex-partner or their ex-partner in front of the children. Keep your differences behind closed doors.
- Cancel on visiting or spending time with your child.
- Bad mouth the ex-partner or their family members.
- Try and buy their love.
- Take things personal.
- If you are responsible to pay child support, do not withhold child support. The kids should not be punished for things they have no control.

Ultimately, very few elements of our lives escape the impact of parenting, even though we may not consciously connect our difficulties, dysfunctions, and issues with our upbringing. My intention in sharing this information is not to shame or needlessly frighten parents, but to educate them in order to spark positive change. The majority of parents want the best for their children, and are themselves victims of negative parenting and erroneous cultural beliefs.

When you find yourself slipping into the bad habit of these negative behaviors, take a walk. Think about what brought you to this place and think of ways to correct it. Think before you speak.

Self-Discovery Challenge:

What are your family goals and values? Are they posted where everyone can see them?

Can your children identify your family goals and values?

What were your family goals and values when you were a child? How do they differ now?

Chapter 4 – Positive Praise

"I'm a success today because I had a friend who believed in me and I didn't have the heart to let him down."
Abraham Lincoln

Parents everywhere praise their kids when they do well in school, sports, or anything that maybe didn't take a lot of effort to accomplish. Did you know that too much praise or putting a child on a pedestal at an early age can hinder their growth? By giving kids lots of praise, parents think they build their children's self-esteem and confidence, but it just may be doing the opposite. Too much praise, and at the wrong time, can backfire. It can cause children to be afraid to try new things or fear not being able to perform to their parent's expectations. In fact, kids who are told they're bright and talented are easily discouraged when something is "too difficult;" those who are not praised in such a manner are more motivated to work harder and take on greater challenges. Those not praised, in turn, show higher levels of confidence, while overpraised are more likely to lie to make their performances sound better. Praise becomes like a drug: once they get it, they need it, want it, are unable to function without it. On the other hand, not giving enough praise can be just as damaging as giving too much.

As a society, we tend to focus on the negative. A teacher marks in "red" the number wrong on a test, instead of marking the number correct in "green". If a child get 97 out of 100 correct, shouldn't the child be praised for the 97 and not discouraged over the three wrong? A coach tells a child how many errors they had on the baseball field. The coach doesn't highlight the number of runs, catches and throws made that were great, he simply focused on one or two errors.

Tips for Giving Practical Praise:

- Be specific. Don't tell your child "you are such a good baseball player," instead tell them what a great hit they had or what a great short-stop they are. Being specific is much better and helps children identify with a special skill.
- Say it when you mean it and be genuine. When you say "good job on that project," this tells children that you recognize the value of their hard work and efforts. It also tells them you know the difference between when they work hard at something and when it comes easy to them. Kids know when you are sincere. If you are not sincere in your praise, children become insecure because they don't believe your positive words.
- Don't give praise where it isn't deserved. If your kids are constantly hearing how smart, handsome, pretty, bright, talented, or gifted they are it will begin to sound empty and have little meaning. Praise children for their effort and hard work, not their inherent talents.
- Encourage them to try new things. Always praise kids for trying new things, like riding a bike, a new food, or learning to tie shoes, and for not being afraid to make mistakes.
- Teach your children to take the "t" out of can't.
- Allow your children to overhear you talking about them in a positive way to others. They will believe you are more sincere.

While there's no secret formula for praise, experts say understanding the where, when, and how of praising children is an important tool in raising confident kids with a high sense of self-esteem. The quality of praise is more important than the quantity. Your praise should be sincere and genuine and focused on the effort, not the outcome.

Self-Discovery Challenge:

After reading this chapter, have you been over-praising your child?

What changes can you make to give quality praise in lieu of quantity?

Chapter 5 – Negative Talk

"No one can make you feel inferior without your consent."
Eleanor Roosevelt

Child anxiety is a difficult situation to handle, and it's one that can be made infinitely worse if you or your child engage in negative talk patterns as you try to confront the issue. If your child has developed acute nervousness over some issue – such as going to school or riding the bus – her frustration can lead her into a never-ending cycle of harmful thoughts that will do nothing except harm her self-esteem. As your frustration with her fears increases, you may also lapse into negative talk patterns – without intending to cause harm. But these damaging opinions – blurted out in the heat of the moment – can make a bad situation even worse.

Things you DON'T say to a child:

- I hate you.
- I don't care.
- Leave me alone.
- Go away.
- Hurry.
- Give me a minute.
- Act your age.
- You're such a cry baby.
- Don't cry.
- You better stop or I'll give you a reason to cry.
- You are just like your (father, mother, sister, brother).

- I'm going to leave without you.
- Why can't you be more like your (sister, brother, cousin)?
- You aren't worth it.
- Don't you get it?
- Do it or else.
- You're so...
- You're bad.
- You know better than that.
- What's wrong with you?
- Wait until your (dad, mom) comes home.
- You shouldn't have missed that ball, pass, or goal.
- You shouldn't try out for sports. No one in our family was ever good at sports.
- You will never go to college. You aren't smart enough to go to college.
- You can't imagine the day I've had – when your child comes home from school and tries to ask you something.
- Great job! Or Good girl! – Every time they do something.

Negative talk has been linked to low self-esteem, poor performance in school, depression, and difficulty in making and retaining friends. So if you want to help your child live a happier and more productive life, cutting negative talk out of your family's dialogue is crucial.

Again, when you find yourself slipping into the bad habit of negative talk, take a walk. Think about what brought you to this place and think of ways to correct it. By staying consciously aware of your thoughts and actions, you will become a better role model for your children.

Self-Discovery Challenge:

We are all guilty of saying things we don't mean, especially in the heat of anger. List some of the items you have said before:

Of the items listed above, how can you rephrase them in a positive manner? For example: "You know better than that" should be rephrased to: "What is another way you could have reacted to that situation?"

Chapter 6 – A Good Role Model

"Example is not the main thing in influencing others. It is the only thing"
Albert Schweitzer

Kids are like sponges, they notice everything. Children have a tendency to model after those they are closest to first unless they make a conscious effort to break the mold. As parents, we should model the behavior and character we hope our children will have and continue to live by the rules that are set. Show them by example and verbal explanations.

Children, in general, do tend to grow up to be a lot like their parents. Social scientists and genetic researchers have identified many cycles that loop from one generation to the next. Children who live in homes where parents smoke are more likely to become smokers. Parents who abuse drugs or alcohol are more likely to find their children someday do the same. Adults who were abused as children may indeed hurt their own children. And that's not all. Parents with a low self-esteem raise children with the same affliction. There are cycles to teenage pregnancy, domestic violence, and under-education. Talk shows thrive on the fallout from cyclical dysfunction.

Awareness of cycles is good. But many of us only dwell on the negative implications. Yes, kids are very likely to mimic our self-destructive behaviors. But, if we do a good job of parenting, it means children also get a lot of good things from us! We know parents with good self-esteem tend to raise children with more secure self-esteem. Parents who succeed in education tend to have children who meet and even surpass their parents' accomplishments. And while it is true that children of divorced families are more likely to divorce, it is also true that children of happily married parents tend to find the same happiness in adult relationships. Why is it easier to believe in negative cycles? The most important lesson that cycles teach us is that role modeling can be an extremely effective parenting tool. It is powerful that we should use it to our advantage. Being a positive role model requires forethought and self-control. Today we talk a lot about disciplining our children. We need to put an equal emphasis on disciplining ourselves.

You should:
- Pay attention to what you say or do around them and think about what kind of example you make.
- Teach your kids about charity. One example is to get involved and take your children to a local soup kitchen or homeless shelter and help serve meals. Explain to them why you do acts of charity so they understand why they should.
- Teach kids about chores by setting a schedule and having them help you. Don't tell your child to do something, but ask for their help. Take time to demonstrate first exactly what you want. The earlier children learn to help, the longer they will be willing to help. *(See Chapter 7 on the relevance of chores.)*
- Listen to them. Utilize the active listening from Chapter 2 on Positive Parenting Behaviors.
- If you want your children to share, set a good example and share with them.
- Instill a sense of belonging by displaying their pictures and family pictures on the walls of the home.
- Avoid favoritism. Surveys show that most parents have favorites, but most children believe they are the favorite. Always be fair and neutral.

- Teach your children about making the right life choices. Allow your kids to experience life for themselves by not making decisions and choices for them all the time. They must learn to live with the consequences from the choices they make. By doing so, it helps them to become good decision makers and problem solvers so that they are prepared for independence and adulthood.

- Reflect on your own childhood experiences. Identify mistakes you feel your parents may have made, and make every effort to avoid passing them on to the next several generations.

- Be the best role model you can by giving up your bad habits. Gambling, smoking, alcohol and drugs can jeopardize your child's future. These habits can create a number of health hazards (including cancer from second hand smoke) or a financial disaster for everyone. Alcohol and drugs can also introduce violence to your child's environment.

- Be careful not to strictly follow the parental behavioral stereotypes of your culture, race, ethnic group, family, or other defining factors. What may have worked for one generation may not work for another.

Challenge yourself to identify the positive things you can role model for your kids — things like happiness, consideration, self-respect, patience, generosity, self-discipline, diligence, kindness, bravery, and compassion. Role model feeding your body with wholesome and nourishing food, expanding your mind with enlightening reading, exercising for physical and mental health, speaking well about yourself and others, and enjoying life with friends and family. Kids respect adults who walk their talk. Children are sensitive and astute with an uncanny ability to distinguish between adults who only talk a good game and those who play the game by the rules they preach. Credible adults inspire kids' confidence and admiration. Hypocrisy disillusions children and sends them looking for others to follow.

It turns out that folk wisdom is right after all because "seeing is believing." What kids see and believe they become. Each and every day, parents build a legacy for kids to inherit. Choose to be a parent who models family traits worth believing in and worth building upon. After all, what goes around, comes around . . . unceasingly from one generation to the next.

Self-Discover Challenge:

In what ways are you a positive role model to your children and others?

In what ways are you displaying negative role model patterns?

For the negative patterns, list how you will make changes:

Chapter 7 – The Relevance of Chores

"No thief, however skillful, can rob one of knowledge, and that is why knowledge is the best and safest treasure to acquire."
L. Frank Baum

Families today are busy. According to Pew research, about 60% of families have dual incomes. On the average each week, mothers spend 21 hours doing paid work, 18 hours doing housework, and 14 hours doing childcare. Fathers spend 37 hours per week doing paid work, 10 hours doing housework, and 7 hours doing childcare. What about the kids? On the average, children between six and twelve years of age spend an average of just under 3 hours per week on housework, and almost 14 hours per week watching television or playing video games. While it is important that children not have to shoulder adult-size responsibilities, pitching in by helping with household chores won't hurt them and may even help them.

Sometimes parents don't involve children in chores because it feels like too much effort to supervise them. If we just do the chores ourselves, we know the job will get done right, and we won't have to deal with arguments or delays. But there are good reasons to go to the extra effort to get children to participate in housework.

First, there's the issue of competence. Housework may not be glamourous but it's necessary, and knowing how to do it efficiently and effectively is a life skill.

Second, there's the issue of values. Insisting on chores sends children the message that being part of a family means pitching in and doing things for the greater good.

Third, there's the issue of personal well-being. Research tells us that children actually feel happier when they make a meaningful contribution to the family. Most don't even find the work stressful.

Below are many ways to get your kids involved in chores without you going crazy!

1.   Pick tasks that are appropriate to your child's age. Be sure to choose simple, straightforward jobs, since most small children don't have the cognitive ability yet to break down a large project into its components.

2.   Keep instructions low-key. Before your child takes on a chore, demonstrate it for him, talking it through as you go. For example, you might show how you sort light and dark clothing into different piles before you wash it.

3.   Don't expect perfection. No child – regardless of their age – will perform every chore willingly every time and will not always perform the chore to your standards (and it doesn't need to be.) Part of the purpose of having chores is to develop a sense of initiative in your child, so try not to micro-manage. It can take a few months for your child to get the hang of helping out, that's okay. It's a skill he can use for the rest of his life.

4.   Use motivation by timing their performance. Give incentives if the chore is completed by a certain time. You can say, "Let's see if you can get it done in 15 minutes and you can stay up 15 minutes later tonight." Or, "The dishes need to be done in 20 minutes or your bedtime is earlier." The incentive reward system is always preferable to

one in which the kid loses something, because it's more motivational and less punitive – you're giving your child an incentive to do better. However, don't turn chores into punishment. You want them to incorporate life skills as a way of living, not a punishment.

5.   Consider giving kids an allowance. If parents are financially able to give kids an allowance, they should. Your child's allowance should also be hooked into their chores – and to the times when your child fails to complete his tasks or has to be reminded to do them.

No one knows automatically how to do housework; we need to learn. Do chores alongside your child to offer appropriate guidance and help. Working alongside you not only helps children develop skills, it also makes chores seem more tolerable. If all or at least several family members are pitching in at the same time, your child is less likely to feel individually persecuted by housework.

Scheduling housework chores in small time increments will be beneficial to everyone. If you spend 30 to 60 minutes per evening doing chores, then you will have the weekend free to spend time together as a family. Put the kids in charge of creating the list or chart to record the chores. Don't forget to offer positive praise on their efforts.

The key is to get these behaviors to become automatic, although kids will occasionally have temporary backslides and that's okay. Be patient.

Self-Discovery Challenge:

Were you responsible for chores as a child?

If your children aren't performing chores, what chores will you implement into their schedule?

Will you use a reward/punishment system? If not, what type of system will you implement to give your children feedback?

Chapter 8 – Basic Life Skills

"Whenever you are asked if you can do a job, tell 'em, 'Certainly I can!' Then get busy and find out how to do it."
Theodore Roosevelt

There is no definitive list of life skills. Certain skills may be more or less relevant to you depending on your life circumstances, your culture, beliefs, age, geographic location, etc. However, there are basic life skills for everyday living and there are mandatory life skills to help your kids not only to survive on their own, but to thrive on their own.

As discussed in the previous chapter, you should work alongside them until you are comfortable with their level of competence with each chore. Some kids take longer than others to learn, so be patient. If we expect our children to grow to be responsible citizens then we need to teach the following top twenty basic life skills.

1. **Respect** – Teaching our kids respect is important. We teach this by being a good role model and showing respect to our kids.
2. **Taking compliments** – Kids strive to do certain things and need to learn how to be noticed for their efforts. They need to be taught it is okay to be recognized for their achievements.
3. **Accepting criticism** – There is a real art to accepting criticism. Sometimes our egos get in the way and we don't want to admit when we are wrong. We need to do a better job of teaching our kids to honestly self-evaluate and change directions when necessary.

4. **Walking away** – We need to teach our children when to walk away from situations that could escalate into violence and/or substance use.

5. **Negotiation** – Today's kids are growing up in an increasingly more competitive world. The one's who will do the best are the ones who are well versed in the art of negotiation. We must also teach our kids not to sign legal documents until they fully understand them.

6. **How to say "no"** – This is important. Not only can people who don't know how to say "no" wind up over-scheduled and stressed, but they will be presented with a lot of questionable options and you will not always be there to monitor them.

7. **How to study** – Start with young school-age children. Many students who do well in high school fall apart in college because they don't know how to study. In college, it's not enough to read the text-book. They need to know how to identify what they're expected to know, what the point of the lesson is, and how to test themselves, preferably multiple times, before the professor does.

8. **How to write and proofread**. They won't have a teacher or parent later to go over their work, so they need to learn the basics.

9. **How to make effortless small talk**. Let's face it, technology has taken over. Children as young as six have a cell phone. Texting is taking over basic conversations. There is limited human interaction. We need to teach our kids how to talk without technology and acronyms.

10. **How to travel efficiently**. We need to teach our kids how to prepare their home while they are away. Have someone get their mail; mow the grass; and have lights on timers so that someone appears to be home. Do they know how to pack lightly? Baggage fees are ridiculous. Do they know how to pay for travel? Are they aware of the hotel, car and airline reward systems they can use? What about making sure the bills are paid in advance, before they go, so there are no late fees in-curred?

11. **How to write a resume**. Recruiters spend an average of four to six minutes on a resume. For many it only takes six seconds to check for key words that would indicate if a potential candidate will be scheduled for an interview. Do they know the appropriate attire for an interview? Can they answer the basic questions asked in an interview? Are they able to effectively match their skills with the skills an employer is looking for?

12. **How to send a professional email**. Many people treat email like they do texting. They use abbreviated words and don't pay any attention to punctuation (or spelling.) Most schools still offer some type of Business class, so make sure you child takes that class!

13. **Basic home and car repair and maintenance**. They don't need to know how to dismantle an engine block or build an ark, but knowing the basics like checking or even changing the oil, changing spark plugs, changing a tire or the battery; and fixing minor plumbing issues isn't just handy and money-saving, it builds confidence. They also need to know how to jump-start a car. They're going to try, even if they don't know how, and it could be dangerous.

14. **How to do their laundry**. Do kids really know how to do their own laundry? What to do when there is a stain? How to separate their clothes and what temperatures to use? Adults might be surprised how many college students don't really know how to do this. Even if they do their laundry now, what happens when they move? Will they know how to use a new machine?

15. **How to grocery shop on a budget**. We want our kids to spend their (or our) money wisely. They need to know how to shop without spending too much. If you are providing the grocery money, consider starting them out with a gift card for the local grocery store for a set amount each month. This will help them to budget knowing they only have a set amount for the month. Teach them how to use coupons and how to use the flyers that display items on sale. Teach them to watch for the "BOGO" (Buy one/get one) items.

16. **Be accountable for their actions**. Unlike responsibility (the "before") and self-empowerment (the "during"), personal accountability is the "after". It's a willingness to answer for the outcomes of your choices, actions, and behaviors. When you're personally accountable, you stop assigning blame, saying other people should, and making excuses. Instead, you take the fall when your choices cause problems. Teach them to tell the truth. Everybody messes up sometimes. Lying about it or trying to cover it up always makes it worse—no exceptions. Ask them: Are you accountable for your actions even if nobody holds you accountable—or nobody catches you? You bet you are. So be your own "accountability cop" and police yourself. On the long and winding road of life, choose accountability at every turn. Have them look to themselves first. Ask four specific questions: "What is the problem?" "What am I doing—or not doing—to contribute to the problem?" "What will I do differently to help solve the problem?" and "How will I be accountable for the result?" Personal accountability is sorely lacking—and urgently needed—in business and across society as a whole. Wait no longer, teach this now. Help them to choose accountability and own their success at work and in life.

17. **Moral behavior, manners, integrity and character:** Standing up for what's right; conscientiousness; and responsibility for oneself and the less fortunate, are all good attributes to have. Although the majority of teens will take risks, lie and break rules during these arousal-seeking years, they will also show remarkable attachment to "what's right" — according to them. By the time these kids reach their mid-twenties, values have shifted, morphed, matured and become integrated into a system that usually reflects a lot of their parents' values.

18. **Dating and relationships**. With some things we will be awkward and fumble when we are learning about how to do them. Dating is one of those things. But it's worth doing, so it's okay if it's done badly, and we can learn and grow from our experiences. Schooling doesn't help

our awkward dating life because it doesn't teach in this domain of life whatsoever. Nevertheless, we can all agree that this aspect of life is very valuable, for this is the first step in falling in love, getting married, and starting a family—and the family is the foundation of society. It is, therefore, important to choose the right mate, know what to look for and what to avoid in a partner, and how to be a good partner yourself. This takes practice and attention to yourself and your date. As with conversation, this experience comes by doing. However, some guidance from our parents, peers and our teachers could help avoid common pitfalls and mistakes that are bound to occur in dating and relationships.

19. **How to survive without technology.** With the advent and popularity of smart phones and e-readers, mechanical watches and books are becoming a rarity. Can our children read a watch? Watches that are "automatic" will never need a battery and will last hundreds of years if taken good care of. One benefit to reading paper books is that older books can still be read, which are usually not in any e-reader form. They can be borrowed, traded, and gifted. They don't need to be charged. They can be signed and annotated. There are no updates, platforms, or file type incompatibilities. I fear that the popularity of e-readers will mean that old books will cease to be read, which will mean that we will be cut-off from our ancestors, which in turn means the first generation in history which will exist as an island, annexed from common traditional humanity in many ways.

20. **Know the Bible.** The Bible is not covered in public education due to the separation of church and state. However, in teaching what the Bible says as an education in history, literature, ethics, etc., doesn't mean state endorsement of it as a religious position. The Bible is the greatest selling book in the history of the world, and in certain households the only education or exposure some students will have to the Bible would be in education. Given the influence of the Bible into western culture and its impact throughout the world, to be denied and potentially remain

ignorant of scripture would be detrimental to a well-rounded, thorough education in its own right. Learning what the Bible contains will put people in touch with what the majority of humanity has also learned for the past two thousand years.

Although a lot of this seems like common sense, many of our young adults are leaving home without this information. Life Skills are disappearing from our school curriculums and many parents aren't aware of the importance of this information. Keep in mind: You don't know what you don't know! You can't teach your kids information you don't have. That's why it's essential that we all stay in a life-learning mode and learn everything we can to be able to pass the information on to our children. What you think is everyday knowledge could one day save your child's life. Don't take this information for granted.

Self-Discovery Challenge:

There is a lot of information to process in this chapter on what our children should know before moving out of our home. Of the 20 items listed, what are your top five?

For each of the five you listed above, why did you select these five?

Of the 20 listed, were there any you were surprised that they were listed? Will you incorporate these into your teaching? Why or why not?

Chapter 9 – Mandatory Life Skills

"One day, in retrospect, the years of struggle will strike you as the most beautiful."
Sigmund Freud

As we discussed in the previous chapter, there are basic skills and mandatory life skills. Mandatory life skills are the skills that if not taught, can produce deadly outcomes. When we allow our kids to be fully dependent on us for all of their personal needs we are putting our kids in danger. Did you know there is a difference between organizing, cleaning and disinfecting (sanitizing)? Organizing is finding a place for everything. Cleaning is removing the dirt, dust and grime. Disinfecting is the process of removing the bacteria and germs (also known as "microbes") to a safe level in your home. Do you know to how to check the dwell times on each cleaner? This is the amount of time that the cleaner needs to sit after application before you wipe it off. Did you know mixing cleaners can be deadly? These are just a few of the items I was referring to that could produce "deadly" outcomes.

Although not a comprehensive list, below are top ten most important items you can teach your children throughout their childhood to help them to live a safe and productive life.

1. **Cooking** - Kitchen safety is one of the most important things you need to focus on. Fires can start easily and get out of hand within minutes. The leading cause of fires in the kitchen is unattended cooking. Stay in the kitchen when you are frying, grilling, or broiling food. If you leave the kitchen for even a short period of time, turn off the stove. If

you are simmering, baking, roasting, or boiling food, check it regularly. Remain in the home while food is cooking, and use a timer to remind you that you are cooking. If you are using a slow cooker, it is still recommended that you stay home while cooking. To prevent cooking fires, you have to be alert. You will not be alert if you are sleepy; have been drinking alcohol; or have taken medicine that causes drowsiness.

Kitchen Safety:

- Never cook in loose clothes and keep your hair tied back.
- Keep your knives in a wooden block or in a drawer. Keep knives away from children.
- Keep your potholders in the drawer next to the stove.
- Turn pot handles away from the front of the stove. Children can pull on the handle and spill the hot contents on their face or body.
- Wipe spills immediately to avoid anyone slipping and falling on the floor.
- Make sure to separate raw meat and poultry from other items whenever you use or store them.
- Do not use the same cutting board for meat and vegetables without washing between usages.
- Wash your hands before handling food and after handling raw meat and poultry.
- Always use cooking equipment tested and approved by a recognized testing facility.
- Follow manufacturer instructions and code requirements when installing and operating cooking equipment.
- Plug microwave ovens and other cooking appliances directly into an outlet.

- Never use an extension cord for a cooking appliance. It can overload the circuit and cause a fire.

- **If your clothes catch fire, stop, drop, and roll.** Stop immediately, drop to the ground, and cover your face with your hands. Roll over and over or back and forth to put out the fire. Immediately treat the burn with cool water for three to five minutes and then seek emergency medical care.

2. **Food spoilage** - Check expiration dates on food items monthly. This includes cans, boxes, bottles, and spices—basically anything you consume. I cannot stress the importance of this enough. Food poisoning can kill you, so don't take this lightly. When you reheat food, make sure you see steam rising from it so that any bacteria are killed during the heating process. There was a new study done in 2013 that found you can still use products after posted dates except Baby Formula, milk and fresh meats. Always conduct a "smell" test and an "eye" test. If the item smells odd or you can see mold, don't consume it.

3. **Cleaning** - You do not have to have a "white-glove" home. General everyday pick up of items is always recommended. You never know who will stop by. The importance of cleaning include:

    a) **Prevents pest infestations:** Organizing and cleaning not only means you can enjoy the comfort of a clean home, but a clean home also helps you prevent pest infestations, as pests are less likely to invade a clean house.

    b) **Can preserve your home's materials:** In some cases, organizing and cleaning can help preserve your home's materials. For example, cleaning your carpets regularly can preserve them and keep them looking and smelling fresh.

    c) **Promotes good health and hygiene:** An organized and clean home promotes good health and hygiene for both you and your family and ensures your living space is safe and non-hazardous.

d) **Can eliminate dust and other harmful substances in a dirty home:** Organizing and cleaning your home can help to eliminate dust and other harmful substances present in a dirty home, making your home a much better environment for you and your family. Dust and Dust mites are the leading cause of allergies and allergic reactions.

4. **How to budget and pay bills.** Even if a student had a job before, that doesn't mean he really knows how to budget money. After all, they've always had an adult to back them up if they ran out. Make sure they know how to budget money for the month and how to pay their bills on time. They need to learn how to track expenses; how to file tax returns; invest for retirement; and save for emergencies. They also need to learn how to use credit cards. Teach them how to understand interest rates, which are insanely high when you're 18 and the only thing on their credit history is the student loan they haven't started paying back yet. Instruct them on when it's OK to use the credit card and when to pay them back.

Basics:

- Teach your kids to "Pay themselves first." When they get paid, put 10% of their paycheck in a Savings Account.
- Keep a good credit score. Teach them how to pull a free credit score yearly.
- Borrow only what you can afford.
- Live within your means.
- Always know what you owe.
- If you make the debt, own up to it and pay it any way you can. Bankruptcy should be your last option, not your first. Bankruptcy will stay on your credit for up to 15 years.

- Pay your bills on time. Mail the check at least seven days before due date. If you pay your bills online, then pay at least three days before the due date.
- Save your spare change in a large container. You would be surprised how fast it will add up.
- Shop around for the best banking interest rates.
- Bills, mail, and receipts can pile up. Go paperless wherever feasible by signing up to get bills and receipts online.
- Invest in a receipt scanner to keep track of paper receipts and keep everything on the computer. Just make sure to keep a good back up of your files.
- Teach them what identity theft means and how to correct it.

5. Basic first aid. Along with the need for learning how to navigate healthcare for yourself and family, also important is the knowledge of rendering first aid and help, such as cardiopulmonary resuscitation, when necessary. Accidents can happen at just about any time, and being equipped with the knowledge of first response is important to the health and potentially to the life of yourself and loved ones. In extreme events, this knowledge could mean the difference between life and death. Often times the response time of medical professionals is too long, and can result in complications and worsening symptoms, which could be preventable by immediate help from a close individual. Looking for appropriate warning signs for things like a concussion, frostbite, heat exhaustion, dehydration, not breathing, etc., would be very valuable and potentially life and limb saving knowledge. Knowing how to apply CPR, clean and dress a wound, prevent infection, apply the Heimlich maneuver, apply a tourniquet, are just a few of the important aspects that could be taught to students in school and have very beneficial, life and limb saving consequences.

6. Basic self-defense. Would your young adult be able to defend themselves if someone were to physically attack them? It's a question most of us don't want to consider, but violence is, unfortunately, a fact of life. Thankfully, regardless of strength, size, or previous training, anyone can learn several effective self-defense techniques. First, remember that prevention is the best self-defense. Attackers, whatever their objectives, are looking for unsuspecting, vulnerable targets. So be sure to follow general safety tips like being aware of your surroundings, only walking and parking in well-lit areas, keeping your keys in hand as you approach your door or car, varying your route and times of travel. Apart from avoiding confrontation, if you can defuse a situation (talk someone down from physically assaulting you), or get away—by handing over your wallet/purse or whatever they want, do that. Hand over your money rather than fight. Teach them nothing they own is worth more than their life or health.

7. Home/apartment – rental/ownership. Whether you are buying or renting, there is nothing more exciting than getting your first place. But there is a lot to do in preparation for this. It can be a really frustrating process, but just know in the end that it is worth the effort. I never realized how much work buying or renting a home could be. There were so many deposits that I didn't budget for. I had no idea of the amount of money that it took for closing costs. It is very important to make sure your child understands what will be involved before making the decision to move out of your home.

Deposits/Fees:

- Electric
- Water/sewer
- Phone
- Cable

- Trash/recycling
- For renting: usually first month of rent, last month of rent, and a security deposit
- Application fee for community neighborhoods or for renting

8. Taking a "time out." Taking time out to do something for yourself does not make you a selfish person, regardless of what others say. You have to have peace of mind to concentrate on the tasks at hand. If you are overwhelmed and do not take a time out, your work and family life could suffer. Stress will not only kill you, it leads to poor decision-making, poor thinking, and poor socialization. Plus, working yourself to death in order to keep up, and not having any time to enjoy the fruits of your work, isn't really "success". It's obsession. Being able to face even the most pressing crises with your wits about you, and in the most productive way, is possibly the most important thing on this list.

9. Time Management. Being able to manage your time is an important personal asset. Learning good time management skills takes time. Benjamin Franklin, one of the Founding Fathers of the United States, had twelve time management habits. Modern psychologists recognize three key elements in Franklin's three-hundred-year-old procedure for changing habits:

1. He started out committed to the new behavior.
2. He worked on only one habit at a time.
3. He put in place visual reminders.

You can use these habits in any order, but whatever you do, teach your kids to work on one each week. Although perfectionism is unattainable, big improvements will be seen and felt in their lives.

Habit 1: Strive to be authentic.

Habit 2: Favor trusting relationships.

Habit 3: Maintain a lifestyle that will give you maximum energy.

Habit 4: Listen to your biorhythms and organize your day accordingly.

Habit 5: Set very few priorities and stick to them.

Habit 6: Turn down things that are inconsistent with your priorities.

Habit 7: Set aside time for focused effort. Make an appointment with yourself.

Habit 8: Always look for ways of doing things better and faster.

Habit 9: Build solid processes.

Habit 10: Spot trouble ahead and solve problems immediately.

Habit 11: Break your goals into small units of work, and think only about one unit at a time.

Habit 12: Finish what's important and stop doing what's no longer worthwhile.

10. Physical fitness and healthful habits: Value self-care in relation to exercise, sleep, eating, health maintenance, and limitations on risk taking, substance use and media overuse. Qualifier: Parents can only control so much, but they control resources, so they can supply healthful food, yank media, insist on full-year athletic participation, and give consequences for problem substance use.

Home is where the heart is, but it's also where a ton of health dangers dwell. We must prepare our children to confront the hidden dangers with caution by teaching them how to identify the dangers. No one can create a 100% safe environment 100% of the time. Accidents are bound to happen, but by using common sense and taking precautions where appropriate, you can significantly reduce the chance of one occurring.

Self-Discovery Challenge:

Although this is not a comprehensive list, out of the 10 mandatory skills listed, what are your top 5?

Are there other mandatory skills that you can think of? If so, list them here and state their importance. Also state how you will incorporate the teaching of these into your child's everyday life.

Chapter 10 – Leadership

"Leadership is not about titles, positions or flowcharts. It is about one life influencing another."

John C. Maxwell

In the last two chapters, we talked about basic and mandatory life skills. Although I could have included leadership as one of the life skills, this subject stands alone. As you will see, it will take many of the basic life skills reviewed to make a great leader.

Today's children are tomorrow's leaders, especially if those children have parents who are leaders. While leadership skills can come naturally, children learn lessons along the way that significantly impacts them later in life. The right words at the right time can make all the difference.

Leadership and Parenting go hand-in-hand. The following are suggestions on how to teach your children to be great leaders.

Both parenting and leadership require vision. As a leader and a parent it's your job to transmit hope for the future, to hold out a vision of success. Your children and your direct reports will look to you for support in making that vision to become a reality. You need to believe that your employees and your children can develop their intelligence and their skills and become productive individuals who will contribute to a greater good. You need to transmit that belief to them. They will rely on you to keep that hope and belief alive even in stressful times. You must be able to create and sustain a positive vision for them which contains the possibilities of all that they can become. You will need to do this through good times and bad.

Both parenting and leadership require passion, determination and commitment. As a parent and a leader you must be committed to the growth and development of your children and your people. This means you must also be willing to make sacrifices to help them get where they need to go. A true leader like a good parent puts his or her followers ahead of himself. Having passion about your family and your work provides the power that's necessary to keep your determination and commitment batteries charged.

Both parenting and leadership require the ability to motivate and inspire children and employees to accomplish their goals. At home as well as at work, research indicates that positive reinforcement rather than punishment is the best way to motivate and inspire. As a leader and a parent you need to understand what motivates your employees and your kids so that you can interact and communicate with them in a way that reinforces their belief in themselves and inspires them to do well. In the process of building teams and families, it's your job to nurture the development, growth and learning of team and family members. One of the best ways to inspire others is by providing a good example. You need to role model the behaviors you are seeking in them, to inspire them to develop the characteristics of an emotionally healthy, productive adult and leader.

Both parenting and leadership require being direct and collaborative. As a leader and a parent you need to know when to give an order and lay down the law holding employees and kids accountable for their actions and when to be collaborative and come to consensus about decisions and actions. As a parent and a leader you will need to allow kids and employees to grow at their own speed, to make choices themselves, and to make mistakes from which they can learn. It's your job to be decisive and to determine which method is at any given time, to project confidence in your choice, and to make sure your actions back up your choice.

Both parenting and leadership require trust and integrity. Your children and your employees need to trust that you will do what you say you will do. They need to feel confident that you will support them and give them what they need. They need to believe that you are grounded and confident, and that you have good boundaries which they can't take advantage of. They need to trust that they can count on you to act with integrity regardless of the situation.

Both parenting and leadership require clear, consistent, two-way communication. As a leader and a parent you need to listen to what your employees and your children are saying to hear between the lines, to understand their perspective, to act with empathy, to encourage and champion them, to set expectations with great clarity, and to give immediate constructive feedback. Your actions need to match your words, so it's your job to listen to their needs, to be consistent in the messages that you give, and to back those message up with appropriate actions.

Both parenting and leadership require emotional intelligence. Whether you are a parent or a leader, you need to be intelligent about emotions - your own and others. When you act with emotional intelligence you know how to control your own emotions and you know how to handle the emotions of others. This requires a great deal of self-awareness and self-confidence. If you don't know how to manage your own emotions you set a poor example for your kids and your direct reports. When you act out or when you don't know how to handle their emotions, it undermines their faith and confidence in you.

Both parenting and leadership require a positive attitude as well as flexibility. As a leader and a parent your kids and your employees will respond better to you if you have a positive attitude, are upbeat and approachable. People respond better in happy environments where they feel safe and respected. You need to demonstrate flexibility and a positive, can-do attitude in adapting to whatever a situation might present. Even during difficult times, they need to know that they can count on you to see the positive and guide them through turmoil. So it's your job to help your children and your employees adjust to changing times and events and to see the good possibilities. Again, your actions are a role model for them how to handle the challenges and changes that are a part of life at work or at home.

Both parenting and leadership require authenticity. Whether you are a parent or a leader, your values impact the people who depend on you. If you are not in touch with your values and living and working according to them, you will send out mixed messages. When we don't operate with authenticity, we don't find happiness and fulfillment. We might end up appearing successful on the surface but we won't be successful in our own hearts.

In small ways, today's leaders can prepare younger generations for their future as business leaders. Each of these suggestions will not only create better leaders, but can help children perform better in school and develop better personal relationships throughout life.

Self-Discovery Challenge:

Were you taught leadership skills as a child? If not, what is your comfort level of teaching these life skills? (Scale of 1-10 with 1 being no comfort level and 10 being proficient)

If you do not score yourself a 7 or 8; who can you enlist to help you teach your children leadership skills?

How can you incorporate these skills into your life?

Chapter 11 - Teach Them to Dream

"In order to get what you want, you must first help others to get what they want."
Zig Ziglar

If you want your children to grow up to be great leaders, they must learn how to dream. A dream is a picture and blueprint of a person's "Purpose and Potential." A dream is an inspiring picture of the future that energizes your mind, will and emotions.

Do you love what you do and do what you love? Are you teaching your children to do that? Do you compare yourself or your dreams to others? When you compare yourself to those superior, you feel inferior. When you compare yourself with those inferior, you feel superior. When you stop comparing yourself with others, you feel empowered. Don't we want that for our kids?

Many parents try to live their dreams through their children. We have moms obsessed with beauty pageants; dads obsessed with bike or car racing; and all other types of dreams that they "wished" they could have achieved but didn't, so they push their kids to do it instead.

As parents we should help our children to transform their dream from a vague notion of an ideal future into a clear picture of where they're headed in life. Many people pursue dreams they have not generated themselves. They structure their lives to meet the expectations of others rather than building their careers around the passion burning inside them. People who allow others to define their dreams seldom achieve anything significant. Lacking an authentic sense of ownership, they give up easily when challenges arise.

We must teach our kids to take ownership of their dreams. They must be willing to bet on themselves. They must lead their life instead of accepting their life – making the right decisions and managing those decisions daily. We should assist them in believing in their vision for the future even when others don't understand.

Here are the top five steps to teach our children for them to realize their dreams:

1. **Clarity** – A clear and compelling dream gives direction and meaning to life, yet often people allow their dreams to remain vague and unformed. The more specific people are about their dreams, the more clearly they understand why achieving it is so important to them. Clarifying the vision reveals a person's sense of purpose. Bringing a dream into focus takes effort, but ultimately only those who see their dream are able to seize their dream.

2. **Reality** – Dreams, by definition, do not have origin in reality. Rather, they are birthed in the imagination through hopes and desires. The more unrealistic your dream, the more you will be tempted to rely on luck to make it a reality. By concerning yourself with things you can control, you empower yourself to succeed, and you reduce the role luck plays in determining your future. Do you want your children's future to be determined by luck?

3. **Passion** – Without passion most run out of steam before they reach their dream. Passion gives you the energy to push past adversity. Passion also sparks initiative, propelling you to move out of your comfort zone. Finally, passion fuels fun. People who enjoy their work

have far better odds of reaching their dreams than do those who are indifferent.

4. **People** – Have I included the people I need to achieve my dream? The notion of a self-made person is a fiction. Every successful person leaned heavily on others along the way. Knowing this truth can free you to admit your need for help and to begin searching for it. People buy into the dreamer before they buy into the dream.

5. **Skills** – Many people live with a disconnection between where they are and where they want to go. They have a dream, but unsure how to make the dream happen. Strategy bridges the gap by identifying the key people, skills, and resources required to bring the dream into being. By translating a lengthy journey into smaller steps, and by creating mile markers to chart progress, strategy inspires action.

Every journey toward a dream is personal, and as a result, so is the price that must be paid to achieve it. By taking hold of a dream it will mean letting go of other opportunities. Along the way, you'll be forced to make difficult sacrifices. Regardless of the unique costs you will have to pay, all dreams carry the price of overcoming fears, dealing with criticism, and working hard. Have we displayed fear or courage in our children's eyes?

Most people stop themselves from reaching their potential. They lose faith in their abilities and begin to doubt whether they have what it takes to achieve the dream. Tenacity begins by winning the battle of the mind, and then it overflows into action. People who end up seeing their dreams come true don't quit when they're tired or when they appear to be stuck. Instead, they press on, past fatigue and through resistance, until they arrive at their goal.

The best part about achieving a dream involved more than what you accomplish along the way. It's about who you become along the way. Seldom do people experience the exact fulfillment of their dream. If you're only content with bringing about the ideal picture of your dream, then you'll be forever disappointed. It is important to find contentment, not in perfection, but in the process of chasing after a noble dream.

Instill in your children that early on in leadership, they want to make their mark. Be ambitious to do something significant, and not allow their drive for success to become a debilitating selfishness. As they mature, they will begin to see the limitations of a life lived purely for themselves, and should make a shift in their focus on adding value to others. They will come to realize that the richest possession is one that outlives us: the legacy of a life lived on behalf of others.

Self-Discovery Challenge:

If your parents or guardians could have dictated your career path, in what profession would they have placed you? What did you dream of doing with your life when you were a child?

In reading this chapter, are you allowing your children to live their dreams or yours?

What actions will you take to allow your children to live their dreams?

Sit with your child and ask them what they dream of being when they grow up. How can you help them achieve that dream?

What positive habits can you teach your children to help them move closer to their dream?

How does your child's dream align with their strengths?

What actions can you teach them to take each day to move them closer to their dream?

Chapter 12– Boomerang Kids

"Sometimes the questions are complicated and the answers are simple."
Dr. Seuss

While most young adults feel ready to move out on their own, reality sets in shortly after they leave their parents' home. There are some circumstances that cannot be avoided such as graduated college and can't find employment, loss of job, economics or illness that may require you to move back home. I know that it can create a hardship on both parties, but if you both work together, it doesn't have to be a devastating experience on either end. Do not always bail your children out of situation when times are rough. Allow them to stand up to their responsibilities.

Definition:

Young adults in western culture so named for the frequency with which they choose to cohabitate with their parents after a brief period of living on their own–thus returning or "boomeranging" back to their original home. This cohabitation can take many forms, ranging from situations that mirror the high dependency of pre-adulthood to highly independent, separate-household arrangements. The term is most meaningful applied to those in middle-class.

On the Positive side:
- Takes financial relief off the young adult. It will allow them to regroup and learn those skills that they were lacking when they left the first time.

- Working parents have more help with young siblings and/or household chores.
- This can benefit parents when they reach old age. In societies where it is common for children to live with their parents into adulthood, such as Asian, and Hispanic cultures, children more frequently take care of aging parents, rather than transferring the responsibility to a third party, such as a nursing home.

On the Negative side:
- Financial and social independence of the young adult may be lost.
- May cause a financial burden on the parents.
- "Empty nesters" may now consider themselves as "crowded nesters."
- Young adults who are able to return home after an unsuccessful job hunt may become more passive in their search for employment if they continue to be financially supported by their parents.
- A lack of motivation can possibly delay the start to a young adult's career and cause him/her to miss months or years of job earnings and experience.
- Where living space is shared, gatherings with friends can be limited in frequency or scope.
- Dating is similarly constrained and can be impaired by the stigma of the young adult's perceived inability to function independent of his/her parents.

Next Steps: You both must agree on the following steps to make this work.
- Have "the" discussion early on to ensure that everyone has the same expectations about the living arrangement. Define why you

are moving back home: to start a career and save money, prepare for more schooling or take a break from everything.

- Set clear expectations by talking about obligations regarding expenses and household chores. Discuss whether dates over for dinner or even to spend the night are acceptable. By setting and enforcing expectations, your parents will help you learn the skills you need to live independently.

- Set a time limit. If your ultimate goal is independence, there has to be a time limit set for how long you can live in their house. Experts say it's best for everyone to be working with the same understanding to avoid the resentment that might arise from unspecified assumptions.

- Pay Rent. For some parents, it will be difficult to charge rent to family. But for other parents, charging rent, even a minimal amount, helps prepare you for living independently and helps parents keep up with home finances. For parents: If you choose, you can set aside that rent for a down payment to assist them when they are ready to move out on their own.

- Hold to agreements. If you hold to the agreements and continue to respect one another, there shouldn't be many problems. Resentment can arise when either parents or children are not doing what they've agreed upon. Keep up the expectations and boundaries.

Self-Discovery Challenge:

What would your parents have said if you needed to move back home?

Would you have an issue if your young adult needed to move back into your home?

What steps could you implement to make the transition easier?

Chapter 10

Would you consider putting aside money paid to you to return to them at a later date? (To use for a down payment or deposit) Why or why not?

Conclusion

"We may not be able to prepare the future for our children, but we can at least prepare our children for the future."
Franklin D. Roosevelt

Parenting is the ultimate long-term investment. Be prepared to put far more into it than you get out of it, at least for some time. Given the stresses of contemporary American culture, the happiness of couples plummets the minute they become parents. And it gets worse before it gets better. In the long run, it is the most rewarding job of your life.

From talking and reading to infants, to making values clear, parents exert enormous influence over their children's development. They are, however, not the only influences, especially after children enter school. It's especially important that parents give children a good start, but it's also important for parents to recognize that kids come into the world with their own temperaments, and it is the parents' job to provide an interface with the world that eventually prepares a child for complete independence. In a rapidly changing world parenting seems subject to fads and changing styles, but the needs of child development as delineated by science remain relatively stable.

How do we help our kids learn to deal with life if we don't expose them to real life? Instead of doing everything for them—getting them on the best teams, doing their homework and shielding them from the inevitable disappointment and randomness of life; get them involved. Are we really preparing them to be "successful"? If they don't know how to tolerate emotional pain, problem-solve, and adapt what will they do?

The good news is that there are simple everyday things that all parents can do to build life skills in our children for today and for the future. Most don't cost money and it's never too late to start.

We may not be able to teach our children everything, but if you can focus on at least five essential principles (faith, responsibility, unconditional love, gratitude and self-worth), it will help them to be successful and feel good about who they are.

Our behaviors are not accidental – most are learned. As parents we must take on the responsibility to teach our children how to be responsible and promote responsible actions.

Starting today, this is your chance as a parent to redefine the meaning of the word "preparation." The preparation needed for the basic and mandatory life skills our kids need not only to successfully survive on their own, but to thrive on their own. If you haven't started teaching your children responsible life skills, it's never too late. You have already taken the first step with this information.

If you feel you need additional help through a coaching process, contact me today at info@michelesfakianos.com. Together we can work through a parenting plan.

Resources

Twelve Time Management Habits by Benjamin Franklin, one of the Founding Fathers of the United States [World Wide Web]

http://www.about.com – This website has a wealth of information on home repairs, car care, appliance repair, plumbing, resume building and other interesting facts.

http://www.cancer.org – This website provides content on smoking and cardiovascular related issues.

http://www.ehow.com – This website contains information for General Home Repair and Car Maintenance suggestions. It is a detailed website however it states that the self-contributions to this website may or may not be correct depending on the subject matter. The content utilized in this book has been verified by a professional in that area.

http://www.fda.gov/food - This website contains lots of information on food handling, food storage, food spoilage and other food related issues.

http://www.pcwresearch.org – A non-partisan fact tank that informs the public about the issues, attitudes and trends shaping America and the world.

www.takeactionwithmichele.com – This website is dedicated to personal growth.

http://www.youtube.com – This website contains "hands on" video demos for many of the instructional items in this book.

Parenting Plan

Index

V

Y

About the Author

MICHELE SFAKIANOS (Sfa-can-iss) is a Registered Nurse, Certified Personal Coach, Speaker and Trainer. She is also a Leading Authority on Life Skills and Parenting, and an Award Winning Author. In 1982, she received her AS Degree in Business Data Processing/Computer Programming. In 1993, she received her Associate in Science degree in Nursing from St. Petersburg Junior College, graduating with Honors. In 1999, Michele received her Bachelor of Science degree in Nursing from Florida International University, graduating with High Honors. Michele received her John Maxwell Certification in Coaching, Speaking and Training in 2015.

Michele is the owner of Take Action with Michele, Inc. and is also the owner of Open Pages Publishing, LLC. Her first book "Useful Information for Everyday Living" was published October 2010 and was later changed to "The 4–1–1 on Life Skills" and released June 2011. Her other books include: "The 4–1–1 on Step Parenting," released October 2011; "The 4–1–1 on Surviving Teenhood," released October 2012; "Parenting with an Edge," released June 2013; and "Teen Success: It's All About You! Your Choices – Your Life," released June 2013. Michele has also written two children's books: Aaron's Special Family and Aaron Bug.

Parenting Plan

About the Publisher

Open Pages Publishing, LLC is a self-publishing company offering books to inspire, teach, and inform readers. We specialize in a variety of subjects including: life skills, self-help, reference, parenting, and teens.

Open Pages Publishing books are available at all major online book retailers. They may also be purchased for educational, business, or promotional use.

For bulk orders: special discounts are available on bulk orders. For details contact our sales staff at:
info@openpagespublishing.com.

If you would like to receive an autographed copy of this book or other books published by the author, please email the following information to:
info@openpagespublishing.com

- Full Name
- Address (street address, city, state, zip, country)
- Phone Number (including area code)
- Indicate which book(s) you are interested in:
  - The 4-1-1 on Life Skills
  - The 4-1-1 on Step Parenting
  - The 4-1-1 on Surviving Teenhood
  - Parenting with an Edge
  - Teen Success: It's All About You! Your Choices – Your Life

- o   Aaron's Special Family
- o   Aaron Bug
- o   Building Leadership Through Self-Insight
- Name of the person the autograph is for.
- Indicate if for a special occasion (birthday, anniversary, graduation).
- Payment methods include Visa, MasterCard, Discover, American Express, and PayPal.